A Church Near You in Wales

An Introduction to Medieval Welsh Churches

written and illustrated by

DENIS DUNSTONE

with a Foreword by

BISHOP ROWAN WILLIAMS

First published in 2024 by Y Lolfa Cyf

Y Lolfa Cyf.
Talybont, Ceredigion
Cymru SY24 5HE
www.ylolfa.com

Designed and typeset in Minion
by Louise Millar

ISBN 978-1-80099-598-7

CONTENTS

A church near you
by Bishop Rowan Williams

'A church near you': the title carries its own message. Wherever you live in Wales, the chances are very strong that you will be somewhere in the neighbourhood of a church, very often a church whose origins go back a millennium or more.

You may or may not be a believer; but the landscape you live in is one that has been shaped by a history of Christian presence and activity. In the chaotic years after the Roman legions left Britian, somewhere around 410, Christian communities provided new focal points for society, educated clerics and rulers alike, maintained links with European culture and slowly but steadily created a new centre of gravity for a flailing, insecure, and often violent environment.

Age of the Saints

Our oldest Welsh churches have their origins in those tumultuous years – the 'Age of the Saints', as we sometimes call the period, even though we have no idea at all of any details of the lives of the Christian leaders commemorated in the names of countless little churches in the Welsh countryside. But as the centuries went on, and the Welsh kingdoms interacted more and more with the Norman rulers of England in the Middle Ages, Wales was increasingly drawn into the mainstream life of the European Church, and some of its oldest shrines became cathedrals in a more familiar pattern. Poverty and political instability meant that the buildings of the Middle Ages were mostly quite modest by the standards of other nations; but all would agree that, modest or not, so many have an austere quiet and solidity that can still make a powerful impression.

This book is a treasury of both image and information about the oldest Welsh churches. We are offered a comprehensive overview of the presence of these buildings in their geographical and historical context, and a lucid guide to the regional varieties of building styles within Wales and how these developed across the centuries. The fine watercolours illustrating the text give a more lively sense of these buildings than most photographs could do, and they are an integral part of the book's contribution.

Lasting care

So this is a book about your neighbourhood. Fully inhabiting a neighbourhood means understanding what has made it what it is – which is why a book like this is so important. And it is a reminder that buildings, however long-lived, are still fragile. Maintaining these churches – especially when no longer in regular use because of population shifts and other factors – is a continuing challenge, and local congregations that are not specially numerous or wealthy can't be left to carry the burden alone. I hope that this volume will create not only a renewed interest but a renewed enthusiasm for the proper and lasting care of what is on any account both a precious legacy and a present gift for us.

National Churches Trust

The National Churches Trust helps to keep the UK's chapels and meeting houses open and in use.

Churches are impressive, exciting and surprising places. Whether seeking quiet reflection, access to critical community services, a warm welcome, a place to worship, or a space to explore, we believe they should be loved and supported. Available to all. Working together with churches of all denominations across all four nations, we help to maintain these wonderful historic buildings and keep them thriving today, and tomorrow.

Our charity has a fascinating history that begins at the start of the 19th century with the Incorporated Church Building Society, founded in 1818 to enlarge and build new churches. In 1953 the Historic Churches Preservation Trust assumed responsibility for the society's affairs with a new focus on helping parish churches in a poor state of repair.

The National Churches Trust was created in 2007 to carry on the work of the Historic Churches Preservation Trust (HCPT), which was set up in 1953. Since then we have helped over 2,000 churches with funding for urgent repairs. Our mission is to support and celebrate churches, provide advice and information, and to speak up for churches of all Christian denominations and the work they do. Our supporters include Sir Michael Palin, Hugh Dennis and Bill Bryson. We were honoured that HM Queen Elizabeth was our Patron throughout her reign.

If you love churches, you can support our work and help more churches stay open by becoming a Friend. Find out more at nationalchurchestrust.org

The Friends of Friendless Churches

The Friends of Friendless Churches was established at a meeting held on 3 July 1957 in Committee Room 13 of the House of Commons.

Led by Welsh journalist, politician, sportsman and polymath Ivor Bulmer-Thomas, the founding committee was a group of friends with a passion for protecting the ecclesiastical heritage of England and Wales.

The group sought to become friends to friendless churches, to "secure the preservation of churches and chapels, or of any part thereof, in the United Kingdom, whether belonging to or formerly used by the Church of England or by any other religious body … for public access and the benefit of the nation."

Initially focused on campaigning and grant-aiding, in 1972 the charity began to take ownership of buildings as well.

Ivor and his influential friends saved countless historic churches – hopeless cases, lost causes – from ruin, neglect and demolition. We are proud to continue their legacy.

We are small charity, just three members of staff, with a big task. We now own 65 churches across England and Wales. We save more churches every year, and the number of churches we are asked to take into our care is increasing.

Apart from a modest annual grant from Cadw and the Church in Wales, we run our charity on membership subscriptions, donations and legacies.

Find out more at friendsoffriendlesschurches.org.uk

Historical counties of Wales

Introduction

This book is a sequel to one on mainly English churches, which included some in Monmouthshire, due to their character and outstanding qualities. Inspired by that, this book seeks to introduce the architecture of other Welsh churches. It is intended to arouse curiosity as to the nature of church buildings and to stimulate a desire to investigate further. The author is not an architect and uses a layman's terminology where possible. The focus is on exteriors, as that is where the history of a church is most clearly revealed. This is at the expense of paying attention to interiors, sometimes with wonderful paintings, screens and roofs.

There are just under one thousand churches in Wales judged to be of medieval origin. With a few notable exceptions, most have been altered over time, some drastically in the 19th century. I have mainly abjured virtual rebuilds and new constructions.

Larger churches normally started as part of a monastery and their dedication was to international saints. Smaller Welsh churches were normally dedicated to a local saintly person. These small churches are often secluded and have become part of the countryside. They have a special atmosphere. More than in England, in Wales the location is part of the church.

The Friends of Friendless Churches and the National Churches Trust have been a godsend.

St Stephen, Old Radnor, is a good representative for Welsh churches, but it does not fit neatly into any of the following chapters. It has a west tower with a turret and a gabled south aisle, a lean-to north aisle (but with no clerestory), and it is largely from the 15th and early 16th centuries. Above all it stands rather alone at 840 feet on the side of Old Radnor Hill, with a view to the north-west of Radnor Forest. This quietly attractive church has the oldest organ case in Britain, and its medieval screen is claimed to be the best in Wales.

Chapter 1: Beginnings

Christianity came to the British Isles from two sources. From about 300 when the Romans were still in occupation, Scotland and the north of England in particular were influenced by Irish monks. At the end of the 500s the south of England was penetrated from the Continent in the wake of St Augustine's mission. These two forces reconciled their differences at a Synod in Whitby in 664, such that in 680 a church was founded at Bradwell on the Essex coast by Christians from Northumberland. Sea travel was the norm at that time and the Irish Sea was a crossroads.

In Wales the earliest Christian activity was in more remote areas, partly for safety reasons, but partly for privacy, hence many of the early churches were in the hills or on the cliff top.

Before Christianity there were religious practices conducted in circular areas marked by a stone wall. There are many of these surviving in Wales which later became used as churchyards. A good example is at Llanfaglan, south-west of Caernarfon. In that role they were called 'llan'. This word has come to mean the whole church, but the Welsh for church 'eglwys' derives directly from the Latin 'ecclesia'.

The earliest evidence of Christian practice in Wales is in the 400s. One of the first locations was Llanbadrig on Anglesey, said to be where St Patrick landed in 440 after a shipwreck. Like all churches at that time it was almost certainly built of wood. The church, as it is today, was built in the 1100s. Like many churches of this age it was a simple single chamber structure, enhanced over time by provision of a separate space at the east end.

Before the Norman invasion there were over 150 Christian settlements, called in Welsh a 'clas', plural 'clasau', and many of these were adopted after the Norman invasion by monasteries. These acted as local headquarters for teaching the faith.

The Norman invasion of Wales was less thorough than the occupation of England. Wales was not part of the conqueror's inheritance and the resistance was strong. So the Normans concentrated on the south and north-east.

Some of the 'clas' churches became Benedictine monasteries but it took more than 200 years to create the network of parishes.

St Faglan, Llanfaglan, was built in the 13th century in a circular churchyard. No longer used for worship, it is cared for by the Friends of Friendless Churches.

St Patrick, Llanbadrig, is older but still in use. It is on the north coast of Anglesey.

St Rhychwyn, Llanrhychwyn, in the Conwy Valley, is said to be the oldest church building in Wales. The oldest part is the south-west corner, including the low-pitched south doorway. Some say this could have been built in the 11th century before the Norman Conquest of England. It was as simple a structure as a church can be. It has been altered since then and the north aisle was added much later.

On the Merionethshire coast, north of Tywyn, is another 12th-century church, St Celynnin, at Llangelynnin. It has a most unusual arrangement of the bell cote over the south porch. It is often confused with another church with the same name but located above the Conwy Valley; this one is sometimes differentiated by spelling with only three 'ns', Llangelynin.

Another 12th-century church, Old Llangelynin, in the upper Conwy Valley in Caernarfonshire, lies secluded among the hills. Originally a single chamber, it has been enlarged over time and given a bell cote.

The 14th-century Church of the Holy Cross, Mwnt, is on the cliff top north of Cardigan. An early site, it still functions as a church though it has been a victim of vandalism. It is a typical example of the early Welsh love of remote places for contemplation.

The original simple church pattern persisted. St Tysilio, Menai Bridge, is a 15th-century church built on Church Island in the Menai Strait. The island is now a burial ground and the old church has limited use, other than as a tourist attraction, as a new larger church was built on the main island of Anglesey in 1858.

St Aeddan, Bettws Newydd, near Usk in Monmouthshire, is a typical small church without a tower but with a double bell cote. Over half of Welsh churches are similar in general layout. This church has an outstanding screen and a west porch, a rare feature more plentiful in Monmouthshire.

St Issui, Partrishow, in the Black Mountains, has provision for two bells and an unusual west chapel, dedicated to its saint.

In the next valley east, St Mary, Capel y Ffin, was built in the 18th century and has a bell turret of a style widely used. It continues to reflect the appeal of remoteness.

Chapter 2: Towers

Capel-y-Ffin introduces the church tower in its most modest form. Over one-third of Welsh churches have a tower. Originally, their purpose was to hold a bell, but there were other uses which called for something larger and more robust. An independent tower had greater visibility, it could be used as a watch-tower, and in some cases it was a refuge from attack. In the east of England they were a waymarker. In some cases, where they were visible from the sea, they have served as navigational aides.

Most are built of stone as this was the most economic and durable solution. In counties such as Essex, with no local stone, brick was used at an early date. In counties with plentiful timber, wood continued to be used, sometimes with a brick in-fill.

The use of masonry enabled an increase in height. Sometimes the tower became an expression of local pride. This was particularly the case when spires became fashionable. Most spires are made of wood, with wood or metal tiles. In areas rich in suitable stone, such as Northamptonshire and Wales, they were often built of stone. This enabled even greater height.

The arrangement for holding a bell changed over time but the basic shape continued. This example is at St James, Llangua, in Monmouthshire, near the Herefordshire border.

This little church has suffered from a lack of maintenance and has recently been saved by the Friends of Friendless Churches.

A more rustic version can be found 1,250 feet up in the Radnorshire hills at St David, Colva. This is said to be the highest church in Wales.

Also in Radnorshire, St David, Glascwm, was a 'clas' church originally, and its foundation has been attributed to St David himself; this may explain its size. This church is painted white like many others in Wales. This, it has been suggested, was intended to make them easier to find, deep in the countryside.

Ninety-five churches in Wales are dedicated to St David.

The belfry arrangements became more sophisticated. St Mary, Llanbrynmair, in Montgomeryshire, is a good example. This was a church founded by monks from a monastery. Provision of a bell was normal from the first churches. Its purpose was to summon and sometimes to sound alarm. Building a tower to accommodate the bells was dependent on wealth and skill.

St Michael, Cascob, between Knighton and New Radnor, has an unusual sloping roof to shelter the wooden belfry. The tower here is independent of the nave of the church.

Unique to the Welsh border country is what is termed the 'border belfry'. This is a stone tower with a wooden belfry above, all under a pyramid roof.

St Cenedlon, Rockfield, near Monmouth, is an example.

Another example is at St Bridget, Skenfrith, in Monmouthshire, on the Hereford border.

A more elaborate version is at St David, Llanddewi Rhydderch, near Abergavenny.

St Wonnow, at Wonastow near Monmouth, has a simpler version. In an area with plenty of timber, use of wood for the belfry was more economic. It also absorbed some of the stresses on the masonry when change ringing began in the 16th century. Some towers had to be buttressed for this reason (see Kerry).

St Michael, Kerry, a 'clas' church near Newtown in Montgomeryshire, has another variant and significant buttressing.

St Beuno, Bettws Cedewain, also in Montgomeryshire, has a more sophisticated variant. Here too buttresses were required, so-called angle-buttresses.

St Idloes, Llanidloes, in Montgomeryshire, is a 14th-century church which was part of a monastery until the monasteries were dissolved in 1536. It is said that the nave was enhanced by the use of materials from the Abbey Cwmhir, over 20 miles away, which, already damaged by war, became a ruin after the dissolution.

Here is another example of the so-called border belfry, quite a way from the border.

St Llonio, Llandinam, in Montgomeryshire, was originally a 'clas' church. The present building is from the 13th century, though modified in the 19th. From the east it has the appearance of having double naves. Access to the turret is by way of a stairway within what is called a clasping buttress around the north-west corner of the tower.

Llandinam is the birthplace of a 19th-century industrialist, David Davies, eldest of eight children, who built railways and invested in coal mining, and became MP for Cardigan Boroughs and Cardiganshire.

St Curig, Llangurig, a 'clas' church also in Montgomeryshire, has its own version of a belfry. This place has the distinction of having a railway built to it in 1863 which never ran a public train, one of David Davies' less successful projects.

The pyramid roof was the first style of tower topping.

This one, at St Matthew, Llandefalle, near Brecon, spreads further than the tower walls in order to drain rainwater away. This is a mainly 15th-century church, though the tower is probably 13th century.

The simple little Celtic-style church of St David, Llanddewi'r Cwm, near Builth Wells, in Brecknockshire, has sat in the early circular churchyard since the 12th century. It has a pyramid roof and Norman windows in the chancel, but the nave has large Victorian Gothic windows. It is a modest little building, but it has been there since the 1100s, and that testimony associated with a beautiful setting makes it worthy of attention.

St Eilian, Llaneilian, on Anglesey, has a very unusual steeple (tower and spire) where the pyramid is beginning to look like a short spire on the 12th-century tower. The nave with its battlements is later, being built in the 15th century.

Bangor Cathedral in Caernarfonshire is a 12th-century building on a 6th-century monastic foundation. Its layout is cruciform, as are most of the larger Welsh churches founded in monasteries.

Its central tower, like that at Westminster Abbey, was never completed. In the 19th century Sir Giles Gilbert Scott considered rectifying this, but it was concluded that, as was the case with many central towers, the structure was insufficiently sound; so the pyramid set modestly low was the result. Such a pyramid built within the tower walls is not usual in Wales.

St Padarn, Llanbadarn Fawr, near Aberystwyth in Cardiganshire, is a cruciform former 'clas' church, founded in the 6th century. Its modest spire is a step beyond the pyramid.

There is a pyramid tower as well as a circular turret at St Cybi, Holyhead, on Anglesey. It has separate aisles for the nave and chancel and is mainly of the 15th and 16th centuries. This was another 'clas' church and is cruciform. A Christian place of worship was established here in the 6th century in the shadow of an abandoned Roman fort.

St Illtyd, on Caldey Island, off Tenby, was part of a priory. After the dissolution of monasteries in the 16th century it fell into disrepair and for a time served as a farmhouse. Early in the 20th century it was bought and became an Anglican Benedictine abbey which subsequently became Roman Catholic and was later taken over by Cistercian monks.

This is an early example of a spire, being on a 13th-century building.

Wales is not famous for its spires. The Priory Church of St Mary the Virgin, Monmouth, has one of the tallest at 200 feet and it is visible for some distance around the town. The church was founded in the 12th century as a Benedictine monastery, but most of the present building is much later.

St Edmund, Crickhowell, near Abergavenny, competes for attention with Table Mountain. This is a cruciform church which originally had nave aisles.

These were removed in a dilapidated state. The spire is wooden and covered with shingles.

St Peter, Dixton, near Monmouth, is on the bank of the River Wye. Its original Welsh dedication was to St Tydiwg. It has a broach spire more common in the south of England. This is a clever way of reducing eight sides on the spire to four on the tower. Part of the nave is Anglo-Saxon.

Being so close to the river, measures are in place to allow for periodic flooding.

Around Brecknockshire there are some churches with broach spires more often associated with Sussex. This example is at St Mary, Gladestry, in Radnorshire, a 12th-century church. The Welsh name is a particular mouthful for the English: Llanfair Llythynwg.

St Michael, Llanfihangel Cefnllys, is a relic from an abandoned medieval town in Radnorshire, near Llandrindod Wells. It has a particularly well-preserved broach spire.

Another broach spire exists in Monmouthshire in what used to be Brecknockshire. St Elli, Llanelly, near Crickhowell, is high up above the River Usk with good views from the churchyard. The tower is believed to have been fortified for defence and it contains a bell from 1440.

St Bilo, Llanfilo, north-west of the Black Mountains in Brecknockshire, also has a broach spire. This is a church which appears to have settled into the landscape and become part of it.

St Mary, Tenby, on the coast of Pembrokeshire, has a spire 152 feet high. This is a large church and the tower is on the south side of the chancel. This may be because the space in the middle of the town was limited.

Grosmont, in Monmouthshire near Abergavenny, was founded by the Normans. St Nicholas church is exceptionally interesting. It has the oldest church roof in Wales, being dated to the 13th century. It has an octagonal tower, popular in the east of England; it is cruciform, and has a continuous roof line over both aisles, more like churches in Sussex.

Inside, the pews have been removed and it gives a good impression of how it would have appeared in the Middle Ages.

Finally, it has a spire.

Llandaff Cathedral is an Anglican cathedral and parish church. The current building was constructed in the 12th century on the site of an earlier church. It has suffered from a combination of neglect and war.

The south-west tower with the spire is Victorian and there is no evidence of what was there before. The Chapter House has an interesting demonstration of how to adapt a four-sided building to accommodate an eight-sided roof. The clerestory of Norman-style lights is not original.

Another means of draining rainwater off the roof of a tower was what is called a saddleback roof. At Michaelchurch-on-Arrow (Llanfihangel Dyffryn Arwy) in Radnorshire, the tower is believed to be from the 13th century. This parish is very close to the English border and, like several parishes in eastern Radnorshire, is within the diocese of Hereford. In this case the tower resembles a large barn, and is set with the ridge aligned north/south.

St John the Baptist Church, in Newton near Porthcawl on the Glamorganshire coast, has a particularly fine tower with an east/west saddleback roof tucked in behind battlements. The church was founded in the late 12th century when Newton was a small seaport.

There is a handsome lych-gate, the purpose of which was as a place of repose for the corpse between death and burial.

St Michael, Llanmihangel, near Cowbridge in Glamorganshire, was showing signs of damp on the north side. This is often the case on the cold north side which cannot be warmed by the sun. This is a more typical saddleback roof aligned east/west.

On an early Christian site at Llanrhian, near Haverfordwest in Pembrokeshire, there is a 13th-century tower with a 19th-century cruciform church attached. The tower is saddleback in form with stepped gables in Flemish style and the pitch lies north/south.

St Senwyr, Llansannor, near Cowbridge, plays it both ways; it can hardly be called a saddleback roof as it is both north/south and east/west. This is an unusual arrangement built in the 16th century. The church has a 12th-century nave and 13th-century chancel. Main access is through a south doorway.

St Mary, Pilleth, stands on the side of a hill south of Knighton in Radnorshire. It is notable for the small size of the tower and its version of saddleback all tiled and orientated north/south.

Pilleth is close to the site of a battle in 1402, not much talked about in England, when Owen Glendower defeated the Mortimer army.

The Church of the Holy Cross, in Cowbridge in Glamorganshire, has a unique octagonal tower the purpose of which is uncertain. It sits centrally on an axial church with a south aisle. It has a turret on the north side.

Glamorganshire is notable for its saddleback and central towers.

Another odd tower is at St Mechell, Llanfechell, on Anglesey. It is topped with an octagonal bell-shaped spire. This is an old church with substantial 12th-century fabric.

St Cynog, Merthyr Cynog, north-west of Brecon, has a very large west tower. It has been suggested that it had a defence role, though the battlements were added later and are more decorative than functional. Its size is mainly due to the thickness of the walls. Here there was no need for buttresses.

St Brynach, Nevern, on the north Pembrokeshire coast near Newport, has an exceptionally large Norman tower. Like so many in the far west, the church was built on the site of a 6th-century original.

Modest buttressing became necessary at some stage. Possibly when a ring of bells was installed.

Most churches with a tower do not have a spire or pyramid roof. They simply have a sloping roof behind battlements and, if they have bells, a turret for access to the belfry. Sometimes the access staircase is within the walls of the tower, sometimes partly separate. All Saints, Llanfrechfa, near Newport in Monmouthshire, is a typical example.

St Gwenog, Llanwenog, in Cardiganshire, has a turret for access to the belfry tucked into the north side of the tower. The crenelations or battlements at the top of the tower were decorative rather than defensive and were fashionable from the 13th century until about the late 15th century.

St Mary, Newport, Pembrokeshire, has no crenellations at the top of the tower but there is a turret for access to the belfry located on the south-east corner of the tower. It also has double gables over the south aisle, a feature described as transeptal.

Towers are in all sizes. St Dyfnog, Llanrhaeadr, near Denbigh, has a short tower, hardly higher than the south aisle. Constructed with sandstone and repaired with brick, it is unusually colourful. It is famous for its so-called Tree of Jesse window, a feature also seen at Dorchester Abbey in Oxfordshire and at St Mary, Shrewsbury.

St Michael and All Angels, Castlemartin, in the extreme south of Pembrokeshire, tucked into a hollow, has an unusual south tower which was at one time saddleback. It was later than the nave but reasons for its location are not obvious. It also had a parvise over the south porch.

Now redundant, it is the 50th church under the management of the Friends of Friendless Churches.

As towers became taller and, with the introduction of bell-ringing in the 15th century, there became a need for strengthening the fabric. So-called diagonal or angled buttresses supported the corners. Support was also needed as the nave became higher and with the creation of clerestories. In Wales, where there was good-quality stone available, this was less of a feature than in parts of England.

St Mary, Cardigan, has angled and diagonal buttresses on the tower and smaller buttresses supporting the nave and the perpendicular-style chancel.

St Mary, Cilcain, in Flintshire, has unusually large buttresses supporting the tower. It is not clear why this was done. The church was built using limestone rubble and this may have led to weakness in the tower.

There are no longer battlements; they have been replaced by corner pinnacles.

In the 16th century towers became more decorative. St Brides, Wentloog, south-east of Newport, has a refined top to the tower.

St Cadoc, Raglan, in Monmouthshire, still has battlements but more decorative pinnacles.

St Mary, Carew, in Pembrokeshire, has an unusual top to the stair turret. The tower is late medieval, and originally had a spire and pinnacles at the corners of the battlements.

In the 15th and 16th centuries towers became taller and more elaborate. St John, Cardiff, is an elegant example.

St Giles, Wrexham, in Flintshire, is unexpectedly fine. Its magnificent decoration and grandeur are attributed to Lady Margaret Beaufort, mother of Henry VII, whose husband had local interests. It is unusual in having a polygonal apse, similar to that at Mold.

Chapter 3: Layout

The simple single-chamber early church gave way in Scotland and the north of England to a layout with two rectangles, one for the nave and the other, smaller, for the chancel. Later a tower was added at the west end. This was the Celtic style and became the preferred style for many centuries in both Wales and England. Eighty-five per cent of English churches are in this style. In Wales, a third of medieval churches have a west tower.

In the footsteps of St Augustine in 580 came a style favouring a central tower and an apse. This is a curved area placed at the east end of the church. In Anglo-Saxon times in England, the tower could stand between the nave and the chancel or might itself serve as the nave. This style is termed axial.

Later, transepts were added by the Normans, making a church cruciform. A high proportion of larger Welsh churches are cruciform, founded by monks.

Other layouts appeared, normally dictated by the lie of the land or by the street pattern, especially in the south of Pembrokeshire.

Layout of a typical Celtic-style church as it developed with a tower, in this case Llangattock Lingoed. East is to the right.

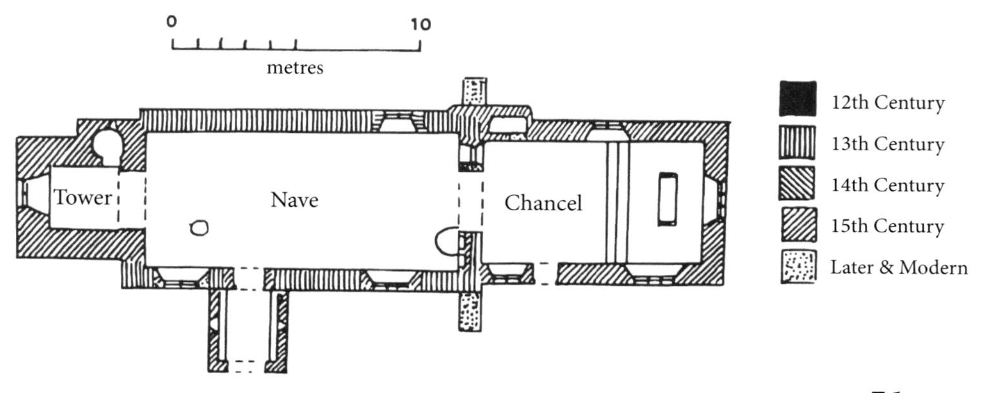

Layout of a cruciform church, in this case Abergavenny Priory. Here there is only a north aisle, but there are two chapels on either side of the chancel. The west porch is a narthex, across two doorways.

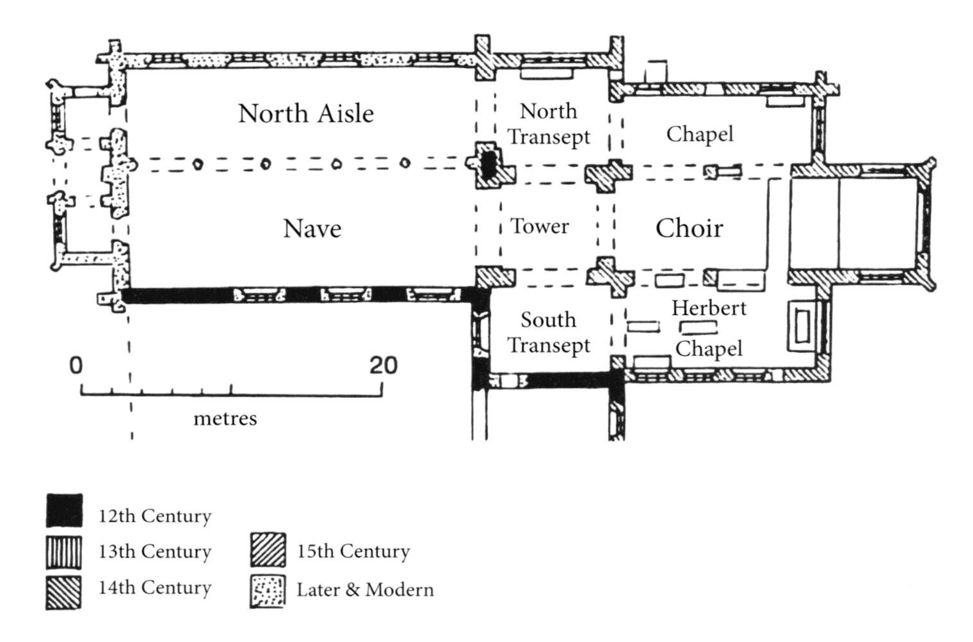

Every church is different but St Cadoc, Llangattock Lingoed, near Abergavenny, is a typical Celtic-style church with west tower, nave and rectangular chancel. There are 295 historic west towers in Wales. Under the Normans this became the standard for the smaller church. The north wall of the nave is supported by a buttress which is in this case functional. Later the buttress became an object of fashion.

More churches are painted white in Wales than in England. The Victorians liked to expose the fabric of which the church was built and therefore removed the render and paint. This church was painted white again after a major renovation.

St Melangell, Pennant Melangell, deep in the Berwyn Mountains in Montgomeryshire, is a 12th-century church in a circular churchyard. The apse is a 20th-century reconstruction of the original. Others were built in the 16th century at Wrexham and Holywell. Other examples in Wales are 19th-century creations. A number of early medieval examples survive in England and they became fashionable in Scotland in the 14th century.

Another cruciform church with a west tower is at St Tudwal, Llanstadwell, on the north coast of Milford Haven in Pembrokeshire. Basically a 13th-century church with a 15th-century tower, it was not intended to be cruciform. as the north transept was added in the 14th century and the south in the 19th.

Squeezed between an oil refinery and a power station on the south side of Milford Haven, St Mary, Pwllcrochan, lies in a sheltered place surrounded by trees. A 14th-century church, it was closed in 1932 and has since been cared for by the oil company. Basically cruciform, with a tower with a short spire on the north transept, it is an attractive little building.

The 16th-century St Winifrede's Chapel at Holywell in Flintshire has an apse. It is another case of sponsorship by Lady Margaret Beaufort. It stands over the well, a shrine for pilgrimages which survived the Reformation.

It is a typical late medieval building with large windows and nearly flat arches, battlements and pinnacles.

St Tydfil, Llysworney, near Cowbridge in Glamorganshire, is an axial church with a central tower. These are rare in both England and Wales, as most of them became cruciform by the addition of north and south transepts. In Wales there are only seven out of a total of 28 central towers, the rest being cruciform. Two-thirds of them are in the south-east.

This example has a particularly large tower with minimal lighting, features which, it has been suggested, point to it having been built with defence in mind.

St Cadoc, Cheriton, on the north side of the Gower, is a fine axial church with a saddleback roof aligned east/west. It was built in the 13th century to replace a church located nearer to the sea and threatened by a rising sea level.

St Thomas à Becket, Shirenewton (sheriff's new town), is a 13th-century axial church but with a north aisle. It is in Monmouthshire near the border with Herefordshire, and the place was created from a clearing in Wentwood Forest under instruction from the sheriff. Hence the name.

St Mary, Caldicot, in south-east Monmouthshire, is an axial church with a north aisle and a north porch added in the 19th century.

St Thomas, Redwick, in Monmouthshire near the Bristol Channel, is another in the chain of axial churches in south-east Wales.

St David, Llanddewi Brefi, in Cardiganshire, now axial, was formerly cruciform; the mark of the arch of the south transept is visible on the side of the tower.

It has an unusual west porch with a south-facing doorway.

St Peter, Ruthin, in the Vale of Clwyd, is one of 21 churches with what is termed a double nave. In practice, in this church there is a nave and a north aisle. Originally this was an axial church, nave, tower and chancel, but the chancel was demolished and a new south aisle built. This now serves as the nave.

The tower stands at the east end of what was the original nave above a vestry, and hence it is on the north side of what is now the nave.

The windows in the spire (lucarnes) indicate that this is a stone spire.

Ewenny Priory, near Bridgend in Glamorganshire, was founded in the 12th century as a cruciform church. The decorative battlements on top of the tower are later. After the Reformation, only the nave continued in use and the north transept eventually collapsed. The chancel and south transept were owned by the parties who took over the priory buildings. Today, like some church buildings in Scotland, the nave continues as a church and the chancel is preserved by the State, represented by Cadw.

St Martin, Laugharne, Carmarthenshire, is a complete cruciform church as built, notable for its buttresses which suggest inferior building materials. The extra south transept on the chancel is a storehouse. Dylan Thomas is buried in the churchyard.

St David, Llanddew, a mile from Brecon, was a 'clas' church and cruciform. The pyramid top to the tower is typical of its time.

St Beuno, Clynnog Fawr, on the north coast of the Lleyn Peninsula in Caernarfonshire, was built in the 15th and 16th centuries and was important for pilgrims on their way to Bardsey Island. A separate chapel is dedicated to St Beuno.

It is a classic late Gothic church with battlements and large windows and is cruciform, though with a west tower. The 76 cruciform churches in Wales are in four categories: those with a west tower with transepts forming a crossing, those with a central tower and a crossing, those with no tower at all, and those with the transepts simply abutting the nave or chancel. This church may be unique among medieval churches in having an entire and continuous transept, embracing both north and south, to which the chancel and nave have been appended.

St Mary Priory Church, at Abergavenny, is cruciform with a central tower, so it falls into category two. The 11th-century church was burnt down in 1403, so the church was rebuilt as a Gothic-style building, one of the largest in Wales. It is notable for its monuments.

St Seiriol, Penmon, near the south-east coast of Anglesey, was part of a monastery. Some of the monastery buildings survive. The church is strictly cruciform with a central tower, and is category two.

St Michael, Llanfihangel-y-Creuddyn, south-east of Aberystwyth in Cardiganshire, is a cruciform small church with a short spire.

St Nicholas, Montgomery, is a handsome late medieval cruciform church with large windows and a fine west tower.

St Woolos, Newport, now a cathedral, has an unusual layout. Between the fine west tower and the nave there is a chapel devoted to the patron saint, as is the case more modestly at Partrishow and at Llantwit Major.

Besides the large number of central towers and the majority of west towers, there are some instances where the tower was placed elsewhere. St Illtyd, Ilston, on the Gower, has a south tower. This may be because of the slope of the land, as the nave was built before the tower. More odd is the orientation of the tower and chancel; rather than being in line with the nave they are directed northward.

The tower has a saddleback roof orientated roughly north/south.

At St Cadoc, Llangattock-Vibon-Avel, near Monmouth, the tower functions as a south porch. This was one of the 'clas' churches and is now in the care of the Friends of Friendless Churches.

St John, Penhow, near Newport, Monmouthshire, is another example of the pyramid roof. This church has a 12th-century nave with a west door. Due to the lie of the land, the tower with a south porch is located on the south side of the nave where there is also a short south aisle. The chimney belies a 19th-century vestry.

St Cennydd, Llangennith, near the Bristol Channel on the Gower Peninsula, in Glamorganshire, has a saddleback roof on a tower placed on the north side of the nave at its east end. This is a most unusual location for a tower. The church was founded early in the 12th century and is largely intact.

The porch is also on the north side of the nave.

St Mary, Nash, near Newport (Monmouthshire), has a fine medieval steeple which has no connection to the rest of the church; it was built much earlier and this may account for its odd position north of the chancel. The Welsh name Trefonnen, meaning 'town of the ash', explains the English name.

Another church with the tower north of the chancel is St Mary, Pembroke. This is a 13th-century church with some 19th-century alterations. The tower was added in the 14th century. The reason for its unusual position may be the result of the west end being close to a street in the centre of the town.

St Elidir, Amroth, is east of Tenby in Pembrokeshire. This is a 13th-century cruciform church with its 16th-century tower also built on the north transept. This arrangement occurs in several locations in Pembrokeshire. Some alterations were made in the 19th century.

St Jerome, Llangwm Uchaf, near Usk, also has its tower inexplicably north of the chancel. It is a 12th-century church with an outstanding rood screen. It is in the care of the Friends of Friendless Churches.

St Elidyr, Stackpole, near Tenby, is cruciform with the tall tower on the end of the north transept, an odd position given the rising land, but good for a sheltered look-out near the sea.

St Mary, Builth Wells, has the medieval tower on the south side of the chancel. This is because the nave is Victorian and, while it was being built, the old nave continued in use.

St Andrew, Presteigne, has a south-west tower which serves as a south porch at the west end of the south aisle. Originally, the south aisle was the nave and the present nave was a north aisle. When that north aisle was pulled down its replacement became the nave.

St Cadoc, Caerleon, in Monmouthshire, stands at the heart of the former Roman garrison. It is a 15th-century church with an earlier south-west tower at the west end of the south aisle. This arrangement was featured in several cases in Norfolk when the original nave became a south aisle after a new nave was built on its north side. Here the tower came first, so there must be another reason for the layout. The church is unusual in having a west door directly into the nave, as well as a south door and a small west door into the tower.

St Mary, Kidwelly, in Carmarthenshire, is a former priory church with a fine medieval spire on a north-west tower. It is not clear why the tower is not at the west end of the nave, but the reason may be associated with the fact that the priory is thought to have been on the north side.

The church is cruciform, but only in the sense that it has two transepts added to the nave and at a different height.

St Nicholas Priory Church, Monkton, on the outskirts of Pembroke, has a south tower on a long south elevation. The priory was founded in the 11th-century and Henry VII was taught there as a boy. The nave of the church is from the 13th century and the rest is from the 15th and later. The monastery buildings were to the north.

The nave of St Mary, Rhuddlan, on the banks of the River Clwyd in Denbighshire, was built in the early 15th century, replacing an older church that had to be removed to make way for the castle. When it came to building the tower it was clearly too close to the river to place it at the west end of the nave.

This is another so-called double nave church. The sketch is after a painting by Thomas Pennant.

St Pedrog, Llanbedrog, lies on the south side of the Lleyn Peninsula in Caernarfonshire. Although the nave and chancel are medieval, the south tower was built in 1905. It illustrates how well the Victorians could imitate the medieval. It has an inside pyramid roof which is rare in Wales.

The lych-gate is more robust than some.

St Teilo, Llantilio Pertholey, near Abergavenny, has a north tower, possibly because the River Gavenny flows along the west side of the churchyard. The church has a complex layout of nave, fore-shortened north and south aisle and, altogether, five small chapels.

St Illtyd, Llantwit Major, in Glamorganshire, has a very complex layout with two churches in one. It began in the 12th century with a cruciform church. This is the western church. The western church has the south door with a very high porch with a parvise. In the 13th century the transepts were removed and the chancel was replaced with a new aisled nave and chancel, the new aisles reaching both sides of the tower, called clasping.

This is the eastern church. It is odd that no clerestory was inserted above the aisle roof.

The ruins at the extreme west end are of a private chapel, as also seen at Newport and Partrishow.

The complexity is such that a plan is called for. This shows how the three parts of the church fit together, from the chapel at the west end to the western church, now a large entrance lobby, and then to the eastern church, which is now the main part of the church.

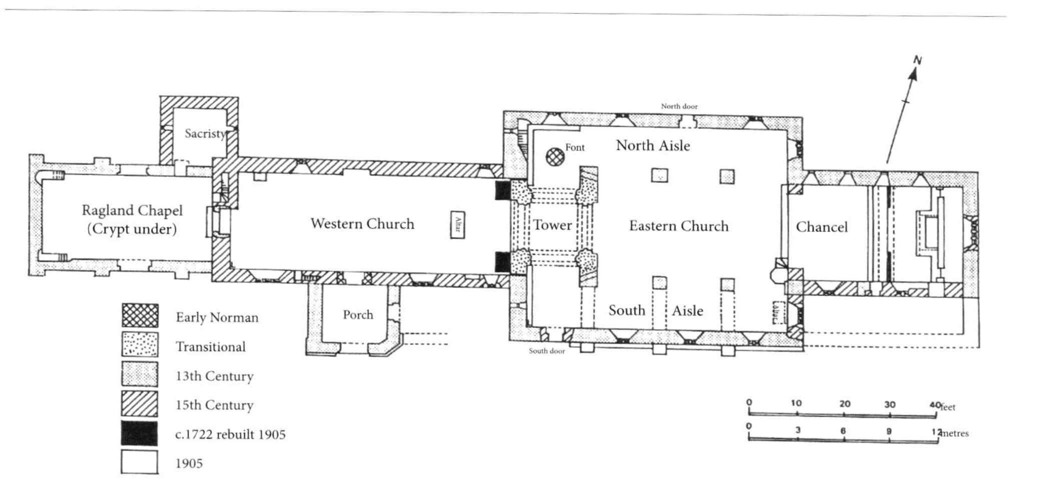

Although there have been cases where a central tower has collapsed or has been dismantled, being replaced by a west tower, there are only three churches in Britain where the central tower has been retained after building a west tower; one is in Lincolnshire near Grimsby, another is in Dorset at Wimborne, and the third is at Bangor. Bangor Cathedral is on an ancient Christian site originating in the 6th century. A Norman-style cruciform building was erected in the 12th century, but this was damaged by kings John and Edward I. The nave was rebuilt in the 14th century and the west tower was built in the 16th.

Possibly the oddest layout is at St Cynllo, Llanbister, in Radnorshire, between Newtown and Llandrindod Wells.

The church was built on a patch of fairly level ground which dropped sharply at the west end. When it came to building a tower, there was nowhere other than beyond the chancel at the east end of the church. Even that required considerable levelling, as the ground rose steeply beyond the church. The result is a most unusual array of windows at three levels on the south side and a unique tower location. The tower itself is similar to others near the border.

Penallt Old Church, near Monmouth, had the opposite problem, with a west tower at the high level and the church descending down the hill towards the Wye Valley. The saddleback tower is east/west like the majority.

St Mary, Haverfordwest, in Pembrokeshire, is built at a high point in the middle of the town. The nave was built in the 13th century, and it was in the 15th century that space had to be found for a north aisle and a tower. It is clear that there was no room for a west tower. The tower has something between an internal pyramid roof and a low spire.

The nave has large upper (clerestory) windows which are not common in Wales. On the south side there is no aisle, but a clerestory was inserted in both sides for balance, and more light.

Chapter 4: Enhancement

As the population increased and ritual became more sophisticated, it became necessary to make more room in churches. This was achieved either by transepts or by building aisles at the side of the nave, introducing an arcade of arches to support the intervening wall. This occurred as early as the 13th century. It necessitated the introduction of windows high up in the outer walls to improve the light. To protect the fabric, these tended to be small. Their size was also limited by the height of the nave roof, because until lead sheeting was available, the roof of the aisle would have to be steeply sloped.

Raising the nave roof could be expensive, and an alternative, more common in Wales, was to erect a gabled aisle which allowed space for large windows, but it did create a gulley which would tend to attract water and debris.

It was a speciality of the Vale of Clwyd to build what was termed a double nave, because the new aisle was the same length as the nave and from the east looked like a double. There was no separate chancel, so only one of the naves was a true nave leading to the sanctuary and altar table.

The only true double nave in Wales is at Bedwellty, high above the industrial valleys in Monmouthshire, where a separate chancel was added at the end of both naves to accommodate the altar.

Other enhancements included pinnacles and crockets (ribbed mini-pinnacles), battlements along the edge of the roofs and the larger windows of the perpendicular style.

ABOVE: The east end of St Sannan, Bedwellty, with the chancel built across both naves and containing a single altar.

LEFT: From the north-west, the tower is at the west end of the south nave.

St Marcella, Denbigh, is the prime example of the so-called double nave, with similar east windows and the same length of nave. The tower is at the end of the north nave which was probably built last. The altar is at the east end of the south nave.

At the east end, St Michael, Rudbaxton, in Pembrokeshire near Haverfordwest, has the appearance of a double nave. The south elevation reveals the deception, with the south aisle terminating at the south porch.

At St Cadoc, Llancarfan, in the Vale of Glamorgan, the gabled south aisle is the same length as the nave. This former 'clas' church has a 12th-century nave, a rather squat but typically Welsh 13th-century tower, and a 14th-century south aisle forming a so-called double nave. The church has some exceptionally well-preserved wall paintings and an elegant wooden screen. There was a monastery here in the 7th century.

St Cynog, Defynnog, west of Brecon, has no double nave as the north 'nave' is in fact only a short chapel. It is thought that the yew tree in the churchyard is some 5,000 years old, which may make it the oldest tree in Britain.

St James, Manorbier, on the south coast of Pembrokeshire, might almost be a 'triple nave' but the north 'nave' is a small chapel.

St Gwynhoedl, Llangwnadl, near the end of the Lleyn peninsula in Caernarfonshire, is a real triple nave with two equal aisles on either side of the original nave. They were added to a 13th-/14th-century church in the 16th century. There is a bell cote on the west end gable of the original church

St Tewdric, Mathern, near Chepstow, has a gabled north aisle with a chancel at the east end of the nave. This is another example of the preference in Wales for gabled aisles. The church is located close to the former palace of the bishops of Llandaff.

The arch in the churchyard is thought to be the remains of a residence.

St Nicholas, Trellech, near Monmouth, was built with tower, nave and aisles in its entirety in the late 13th century. As a result, it was possible to have a roof sufficiently high to accommodate the sloping aisle roof and clerestory windows. At that time Trellech was a relatively important town and larger than Cardiff.

Similarly, St Mary, Llanaber, near Barmouth in Merionethshire, on the west coast, was built with aisles and clerestory early in the 13th century. It is held up as a perfect example of what is called Early English style; it is in the first Gothic style, plain and simple, with pointed arches to doors and windows. During the 13th century it superseded the Norman which was Romanesque, with round arches and tops to doors and windows.

St Mary, Beddgelert, in Caernarfonshire, was built in the 13th century as part of an Augustinian priory, but there has been Christian activity on the site since the 6th century. The building has some distinctive Early English-style lancet windows at the east end, particularly deep.

On the other hand, at St Aelhaiarn, Guilsfield, just north of Welshpool in Montgomeryshire, it was necessary to raise the height of the nave in the 16th century in order to accommodate the larger clerestory windows and the slope of the aisle roof. The ridge of the nave, in fact, partly blocks a belfry opening. If lead sheeting had been used for the aisle roof, it might have been possible to have a lower slope and avoid raising the height of the nave. However, the weather in Wales is wetter than it is in Suffolk and good drainage is probably more important.

There is a double-storey south porch with what is called a parvise. The short spire resembles what is called a Hertfordshire spike.

When Cistercians founded the abbey in the 12th century there was no town, but fortifications were built to protect it. St Mary and All Saints Church, Conwy, Caernarfonshire, became the town church. In the 16th century the aisle roofs were raised and in the 19th century the nave roof had to be raised to better accommodate the modest clerestory.

Alterations to churches have not always been to enlarge them. St Mary, Llanfair-ar-y-Bryn, near Llandovery in Carmarthenshire, is a 12th-century church with a 15th-century tower. In the 18th century, an already ruinous south chapel was demolished. The scars remain in the south wall.

St Chad, Holt, in Flintshire, looks very English. Perhaps this is not surprising as it is close to the banks of the River Dee, which at this point marks the border. It also belies the earlier comment that Welsh weather requires steeper slopes to roofs. The aisle roofs have a very shallow slope, and there is no clerestory. There are, however, exceptionally large perpendicular-style windows. It seems likely, therefore, that raising the earlier nave roof to make room for a clerestory was judged unnecessary.

This is a good example of the perpendicular style which was developed from about 1350, inspired by the choir of Gloucester Cathedral. It was unique to England and Wales.

All Saints, Gresford, near Wrexham, also in Flintshire, is another late medieval church built in the perpendicular style with large windows and nearly flat arches. At Gresford the slope of the roof over the aisles is nearly flat, easily allowing space for a clerestory.

St Mary, Mold, in Flintshire, is another church sponsored by Lady Margaret Beaufort. It has similar characteristics to Gresford, Holt and Wrexham. Perhaps, in imitation of Wrexham, an apse was placed at the east end in the 19th century by Sir Giles Gilbert Scott. The lights in the clerestory are minimal but presumably considered sufficient.

It has a most unusual flight of steps leading up to the south porch.

In contrast with the search for light in the later Middle Ages, at St Odoceus, Llandawke, near Laugharne in Carmarthenshire, the windows are minimal. It has a pyramid roof which is elegantly curved. This little 13th-century church is now in the care of the Friends of Friendless Churches.

There was a monastery on the site in the 7th century, which must have had some status, because William the Conqueror took the trouble to visit it in 1081.

St Davids Cathedral was consecrated in the 12th century under the Normans who negotiated with the Pope to make it a place of pilgrimage. The central tower of the cruciform building collapsed twice in the 13th century, and in the 14th century it was restored and additions were made to the nave and choir.

The tower retained its Norman character and the clerestories over both nave and choir remained distinctively Romanesque. Elsewhere, later larger Gothic window forms appeared.

One of the characteristics of Welsh churches is the preference for the gabled aisle. As has been demonstrated, the typical double nave is in fact a nave and a gabled aisle and this practice is not confined to the Clwyd Valley. St John, Cardiff, demonstrates the liking for the gabled aisle. The medieval building had gabled aisles on both the chancel and nave.

Tintern Abbey, on the River Wye in Monmouthshire, was built mainly in the 13th century and has a roof high enough to accommodate large clerestories over lean-to aisle roofs. Founded as a Cistercian abbey by the de Clare family, this is another case of gradual decay after the dissolution of monasteries; that is now happily arrested. This is another cruciform church originally, with aisles to both nave and chancel.

Brecon Cathedral was originally a monastery church started in the 13th century. A substantial part of the original monastery buildings survives, now in use as diocesan offices. It is a cruciform building with Early English lights (tall, narrow and pointed) in the chancel and transepts. The north aisle has a most unusual gabled window set into the slope of the lean-to roof to illuminate the chapel below.

St Crallo, Coychurch, near Bridgend in Glamorganshire, is a near perfect cruciform church from the 13th century. It has minimal clerestory windows in contrast to the previous two examples.

St Edward, at Knighton on the Radnorshire/Herefordshire border, has a larger clerestory with a row of simple early Gothic windows. It is one of the border churches with the characteristic belfry, and it looks as though it has a rather cramped parvise over the porch.

It was not always considered necessary to insert a clerestory. In the case of St Tysul, at Llandysul in Cardiganshire, the wide aisles were given enough windows to provide an adequate amount of light. This is a church with a north doorway entrance.

In areas where there was plentiful timber, it was easier to extend the roof than to build walls. At St Michael, Mitchel Troy, near Monmouth, the roof of the nave was extended over the south aisle in a style reminiscent of churches in Sussex. Two dormer windows were inserted in the south side of the nave roof. They were needed because the aisle windows were small and the west tower blocked light into the nave.

Chapter 5: Doorways

Most Welsh churches have a south doorway with a porch. There are few examples with a north door but, unlike England, there are a greater number of west doorways, with or without a porch.

The reasons for doors leading into the nave rather than at the west end facing the altar probably lie in myth and primitive beliefs about the devil. He occupied the cold north side of a church and at baptism needed an escape door on the north side. In England there are many examples of the existence of both north and south doors, but this occurs less in Wales.

The porch is a feature of cooler countries. In Scandinavia they are called the 'weapon house', the place to disarm. Here they are a protection from the weather and have been used for marriages and meetings. From the 14th century onwards, a second-floor chamber, a parvise, was introduced and in some cases was even used to house the curate.

It is notable that the use of a west door is much less in Britain than on the Continent. The exception is Nonconformist chapels, and abbeys and cathedrals with twin towers, such as Llanthony.

Just south of Penarth in Glamorganshire, St John, Sully, is unusual. Some ten per cent of medieval Welsh churches have a south porch and more than half have a south door. But it is exceptional for that door to be in the tower.

More common is a south tower built to contain the porch, as at Llangattock-Vibon-Avel.

There is also a small priest's door into the chancel, again on the south side.

The reason for the preference for the south side may be attributable to the fact that the colder north side was at one time held to be the devil's side.

St Andrew, Penrice, has a nave and chancel from early in the 12th century. Penrice was the largest town in the Gower and it is likely that the large size of the south porch, in fact a south transept, was built for the purpose of conducting meetings and, for a time, a school.

The church is cruciform in the sense that it has two transepts, but that is incidental. The north transept is the vestry.

St Cadwg, Llangattock, near Crickhowell, has two south porches. In this case the priest's door into the chancel, which is usually discretely tucked away, also has one.

St Bridget, St Brides Major, in Glamorganshire, has a porch only on the north side, probably because of ease of access.

St Mael and St Sulien, Corwen, in Merionethshire, has been much altered in the 19th century but retains a north doorway facing the most convenient direction of access. The south doorway has been converted into a vestry.

The site of St Teilo, Llandeilo, in Carmarthenshire, has been a Christian location since the 6th century and was at one time the seat of a bishop. The present church was rebuilt in the 19th century, though the tower is from the 16th century. The steep slope on the south side of the church explains why it is entered by a north door.

At St Cewydd, Aberedw, south of Builth Wells, but in Radnorshire, the north door has a remarkable porch with an oak leaf decoration. On the south side the priest's door has been blocked up, and in the 19th century a door was inserted in the tower.

St Mary Magdalene, Kenfig, in Glamorganshire, has an unusual west porch. There are 11 of these in neighbouring Monmouthshire and four in Glamorganshire, and this is more than anywhere else in Wales. In England it is likely that the use of a west door into a tower was discouraged because of possible interference with bell ringing, but although that is less important in Wales, there should be a reason. Possibly, Norman influence encouraged the practice, but there is no firm evidence for this, and the shortage of west doors on even central towered churches raises a doubt.

This church also has a unique outside stairway to the belfry and has an east/west saddleback roof.

St David, Manordeifi, in Pembrokeshire, is close to the River Teifi, which here forms the border with Cardiganshire. Members of the congregation from that side were ferried across the river in a coracle. One of these is kept in the west porch. This owes its odd shape to its southward enlargement to accommodate a memorial. Built originally in the 13th century, the church ceased to be a parish church in 1899 as, due to flooding, a new church was built further from the river. It became a chapel. It is now in the care of the Friends of Friendless Churches.

Near Grosmont, in Monmouthshire, St Teilo, Llantilio Crossenny, is another church with access through an unusually large west porch. It also has a spire which was added in the 18th century. This is a large cruciform church for a small village.

St Lawrence, Gumfreston, is in Pembrokeshire, near Tenby. This is a church with nave and chancel little altered since construction in the 12th century. It has a large west porch and the typically Pembrokeshire tower was built on the north transept in the 15th century. It was a cruciform church in that it had two small transepts. The church is located in a wooded valley close to historic wells and has suffered from damp. Wall paintings have been discovered by the Friends of Friendless Churches while they were conducting a major restoration programme.

St Asaph Cathedral is a cruciform central towered church with nave aisles. There is a small clerestory and a very fine west doorway, though without a porch. Modest and unassuming, but colourful, it is the smallest cathedral in Britain, and is a classic large church.

It has a notable use of gabled buttresses, more decorative than supportive, and a small clerestory.

This is the west front of Margam Abbey, Glamorganshire, as it appeared in 1786, before the addition of two pillars on the buttresses and the removal of a wall. There was originally a porch over the west door.

The priory church of St Mary, Abergavenny, has an unusual west entrance in what is called a narthex. This is a feature more common on the Continent and in Nonconformist chapels.

This is another cruciform church with a central tower.

Monmouthshire has a high proportion of west doors.

The ruined priory church at Llanthony, north of Abergavenny, deep in the Black Mountains, is the only church in Wales to have twin west towers. As seen at Llandaff Cathedral, this was a common formula for both cathedrals and abbeys in England and also occurred in Scotland. The main entrance was normally between the towers. At Llanthony both towers were originally taller.

Built in the 13th century, it has both Romanesque and Gothic spaces.

The church became a ruin when it was deserted after the dissolution and the south-west tower is now part of a hotel.

St Hywyn, Aberdaron, near the end of the Lleyn Peninsula, was a 'clas' church and monastery, the present building dating from the 12th century. It was important for pilgrims as it was near the harbour and boats to Bardsey Island. The original single nave has a Romanesque doorway at the west end. The proximity of the sea no doubt discouraged the construction of a south door and an additional door was constructed at the east end of the north wall. A second nave or south aisle was added in the 16th century. Surprisingly, this was between the original nave and the sea.

Another church with only a west door entry is St Mary, Llanfair-yng-Nghornwy, in north-west Anglesey. This is an early church with a 11th- or 12th-century nave. The tower is later and has a most unusual arrangement for the single bell; it is suspended in a niche below one of the battlements on the west side. Similar to Llanpadarn, the tower has a small pyramid roof inside the battlements that is more like a short spire. It has no south doorway as the south porch was converted into a vestry. Beyond an arcade on the south side of the chancel, there is a 16th-century chapel.

St Decumanus, Rhoscrowther, Pembrokeshire, has an unusually large north porch. It is cruciform in the sense that it had transepts, but they were adjacent to the nave, not the tower. With a 13th-century nave, a tower was built later on the south transept. This church is also uncomfortably close to an oil refinery. In 2005 an explosion caused some damage to the roof and the church was closed. It is another in the care of the Friends of Friendless Churches.

St Lucia, Llanwnnen, near Lampeter in Cardiganshire, has more Victorian components than most of the churches in this book, but is of interest as an example of a church with only a west door.

The 19th-century tower was built without a turret or staircase as there are no bells.

It has what are termed crow-stepped crenellations, a fashion which developed in the later Middle Ages.

In England the tower west door (if there was one) was often ignored, possibly due to the bell ringers being an obstruction. There is less evidence of this in Wales, though St Peter, Carmarthen, has a south porch and doorway closed up, and a west door in use with the bell ringers out of the way on an upper floor. Here the west door is approached through a lych-gate and is the most conveniently placed entrance.

St Mary, Beaumaris, on Anglesey, has a parvise over the south porch. It is unclear what prompted this development which spread across the whole of Britain from the 14th century. They were used for weddings, meetings, official business and, in some cases, as a residence for junior clergy. Latterly they have become a useful place to put things.

Close to the Severn estuary, St Mary, Magor, in Monmouthshire, is an axial church and has a parvise over the north porch. This is an unusual church as it is internally cruciform. In other words, it has chambers adjacent to the tower north and south, at the end of the short nave aisles. There is a better example of this with a parvise at Southwold in Suffolk.

St Mary, Welshpool, also has a parvise. The south side of the nave has three large windows put in during the 19th century, but the parvise is from the 15th century.

The parvise was sometimes a very modest affair. At St Engan, Llanengan, Caernarfonshire, the church was expanded just before the Reformation in the 16th century. Situated on the south coast of the Lleyn peninsula, it was an important church for pilgrims on their way to Bardsey Island.

The south porch has stone benches on either side and was clearly a resting place.

The raised extension in the angle of the tower and south aisle is in connection with the provision of a latrine.

At St Ishmaels, St Ishmael, the parvise is even more modest. On a south-facing porch with an east/west saddleback roof, it is almost certainly unique. This church is close to Milford Haven in Pembrokeshire.

Chapter 6: Casualties and Curiosities

Churches are, like any buildings, vulnerable. Some have been victims of war and religious strife, others of poor construction materials and population movement. In north Monmouthshire severe earth movement has produced odd results, as at Cwmyoy. Some have suffered from flooding, especially if near the River Severn. Some have been simply neglected.

Most have been altered over time. It is rare for a church such as Llanaber to survive intact unaltered for 700 years.

An area of vulnerability is the crossing under a central tower. Weakness or collapse has led to many changes in English churches, but there is clearly much less risk if the transepts are tacked onto an existing nave, rather than there being a heavy tower suspended on arches. Some of the more interesting casualties have led to clever adaptations, as at Chepstow and Ruthin.

Although there is a greater interest today in conservation, it takes local initiative and enthusiastic individuals to save old buildings no longer used. The Friends of Friendless Churches has been a godsend.

More a curiosity than a casualty, St Tydecho, Mallwyd, in Merionethshire, is unconventional. Its wooden tower is unusually high and most of the windows are dormers. There is the tusk of a primeval mammal across the doorway. The first church on the site was in the 6th century but the present building is from the 14th. This is where John Davies, a leading Welsh intellectual of the Renaissance, was vicar for 30 years.

The Church of the Holy Martyrs, Mathry, south of Fishguard in Pembrokeshire, is a 19th-century construction on the site of a medieval church. It is included here because of its singularly unusual character. The south entrance is in a south tower which has a diagonal extension, and there is an apse.

St Martin, Cwmyoy, in the Llanthony valley in Monmouthshire, was the victim of an earth-slip. Whether the cause was a slight earthquake or simply heavy rain is unknown. A similar slip occurred a few miles away on the Skirrid Mountain, alleged to have occurred on the day of the Resurrection. A Roman Catholic chapel once stood on the top of the mountain which became known as the Holy Mountain.

At St Martin, the nave is standing vertical, but the chancel and tower lean in opposite directions. The tower is supported by enormous buttresses. Yet it still functions.

St Michael, Llanfihangel Crucorney, went through a bad patch but eventually emerged. In 1835 the nave was pulled down as the roof was unsafe. It was rebuilt but with a temporary roof. By 1974 this roof was unsafe, and following an earth tremor part was pulled down. The walls remained standing and until 2004, half of the nave remained open to the elements. A Lottery grant enabled repair.

Behind looms the Skirrid Mountain.

There are 77 Llanfihangels in Wales.

Just north of Swansea, St David, Llangyfelach, suffered a similar problem from the weather. A storm in 1803 caused the total collapse of the nave and chancel of the church and it was decided to rebuild them lower down the hill. As a result, the west tower stands detached.

There are two other detached towers in Wales but they are generally judged to have been, deliberately so, either defensive or as a refuge.

St Sadwrn, Henllan, near Denbigh, was a 'clas' church and is another unusual case with a detached tower. The reason for this is unknown. Speculation suggests that its position on an outcrop of rock was to give it prominence. The rest of the church was much altered in the 19th century.

St Mary (Yr Hen Gapel), Llanybri, was a chapel-of-ease to nearby Llansteffan in Carmarthenshire. Sometime around 1670, it seems that it had become part ruined. It was taken over by a Nonconformist group, who repaired it and used it until 1962. It was listed Grade II in 1966, but a fire caused serious damage in 1974 and only the tower and east end wall have survived.

This was a rare example of a Catholic or Church of England or Church of Wales church being taken on by Nonconformists.

St Mary, Newtown, in Montgomeryshire, stands on the south bank of the River Severn. This river is notoriously prone to flooding and the church was too close to it. In 1856 a new church was opened further from the river and large enough to hold the congregation. St Mary was left to collapse. The ruin has been stabilised since 1939.

St Cwyfan, Aberffraw, on Anglesey, had a happier outcome after suffering near disaster. A rise in sea level caused the church which stood near the beach to become flooded at high tide. It was abandoned in favour of a church further inland. However, in 1893 a local architect raised money to build a wall around the church. This kept the sea out, even at high tide, and the church is now used again, though access is only at low tide.

When Llandrindod Wells in Radnorshire expanded in the 19th century with the arrival of the railway, Holy Trinity, the old church, became sidelined on the hill outside the town. A new church in the town was consecrated in 1881. In order to persuade people to use the new church, the Archdeacon of Brecon had the roof of the old church removed. In 1894 there was a change of heart, or a change of Archdeacon, and the fabric of the old church was used to build a replacement, confusingly also dedicated to the Holy Trinity.

The Benedictine priory at Usk, in Monmouthshire, was founded in the mid-12th century by the de Clare family; Elizabeth de Clare was later the founder of Clare College, Cambridge. In the 15th century, the priory was destroyed during the Glendower uprising and in 1536 it was dissolved by Henry VIII. St Mary became the parish church, but, as part of the Reformation, the chancel and transepts were destroyed, together with most of the other priory buildings. The former cruciform church became axial with a north aisle. Without a chancel, the tower became used in its place.

An unusual feature is the west porch, which is on the west end of the north aisle, which also has a north porch.

St Mary, Caernarfon, was built into the north-west corner of the town walls in the early 14th century. Its purpose was to provide a church for the garrison occupying King Edward I's newly constructed castle. The round tower of the town wall was given a bell cote and formed the north-west corner of the church, providing space for a vestry. The sketch shows the north wall of the church and, through the arch, part of its east end.

The former priory church of St Mary, Chepstow, also in Monmouthshire, has had a difficult history.

Originally central towered and cruciform, the chancel was demolished during the Reformation. In 1701 the central tower fell down, destroying the transepts. In 1706 the west end of the nave was converted into a tower incorporating the great Norman west door and adding two stages.

In the 19th century the aisles were removed, the arcades were blocked up, and a chancel was built together with a south transept. The Norman clerestory survived.

Central towers proved vulnerable where they were supported on arches at a crossing and there were several examples of this in England.

There are 155 churches in Wales dedicated to St Mary.

St Cadfan, Tywyn, in Merionethshire, also had a stormy past. The fine Romanesque nave was built with aisles and a minimal clerestory in the 12th century, and the church became cruciform in the 14th. In 1693 the tower collapsed damaging the chancel and destroying the south transept. In 1737 a new tower was built, but at the west end of the nave. In 1884 it was pulled down and a central tower was erected. It is now a cruciform church again, of various ages and with a Norman nave.

Tywyn is better known in railway circles as Towyn, headquarters of the Talyllyn Railway.

The Old Church of St Nidan, at Llanidan, on Anglesey, built in the 14th century, was on the site of an earlier church from the 7th century. It acquired a second nave or north aisle in the 15th century and was for a time one of the largest churches on the island. It became ruinous at its west end and it was decided in 1839 to build a new church elsewhere. It was partly demolished in about 1844, though it continued in use as a mortuary chapel. Ironically, the west wall and turret, the part in the worse state, survived.

Later, the local landowner partially restored it. A new east wall was built at the point of the second arch in the arcade, leaving the rest of the arcade outside. This strange arrangement survives.

Disasters are not confined to periods of climate change. In 1859 the Great Storm, with waves 15 feet above high water, destroyed much of St Brynach church at Cwm-yr-Eglwys. Only the west end survives at the edge of the beach. This is a normally sheltered east-facing bay on the north coast of Pembrokeshire, near Newport. Its tranquillity is normally reinforced by the Dinas Head peninsula to the west.

The level of the sand has since risen and a sea wall was put in after the storm.

At the southernmost point on the coast of Pembrokeshire, St Govan's Chapel snuggles into the side of the cliff. It is reached by steps from the cliff-top. Now more a curiosity for tourists than a holy site, it is said to have been founded in the 6th century by St Govan who lived in an adjacent cave.

Old Church of St Peter, Llanbedr Dyffryn Clwyd, in Denbighshire, was replaced by a new church in 1864. It had been showing signs of wear and its graveyard was full. It became disused and gradually became ruinous. It was not until 1973 that a Friends of Old St Peter's was formed to arrest decline. It was finally deconsecrated in 1991.

A similar fate, but with a human contribution, hit St Mary, Caerau, near Cardiff. An east/west saddleback church from the 13th century, it was closed in 1973. Its subsequent deterioration has been rapid, mainly in this case due to vandalism. A group of volunteers has formed the Friends of St Mary's with the intention of arresting the decay.

This could happen to a church near you.

Statistics

The official total number of medieval-origin churches in Wales is:

Pembrokeshire: 150
Monmouthshire: 132
Glamorganshire: 110
Carmarthenshire: 85
Brecknockshire: 74
Cardiganshire: 71
Caernarfonshire: 70
Anglesey: 69
Denbighshire: 62
Radnorshire: 60
Montgomeryshire: 56
Merionethshire: 34
Flintshire: 30

Of the total 951, half are in the counties with a coastline on the Bristol Channel.

This figure includes total rebuilds on old foundations. This book has 183 of them, all except two with a significant proportion of original medieval fabric.

INDEX *Locations listed by county*

GLAMORGANSHIRE

MERIONETHSHIRE

MONMOUTHSHIRE

MONTGOMERYSHIRE

PEMBROKESHIRE

RADNORSHIRE